KU-310-552

Rajasthan

© **Lustre Press Pvt. Ltd. 1995**

All rights reserved. No part of this publication may be reproduced or transmitted in any form or by any means without prior permission from the publishers

ISBN: 81-7437-035-8

Rajasthan

KISHORE SINGH

Lustre Press

Delhi ◆ Banaras ◆ Agra ◆ Jaipur ◆ The Netherlands

No more spectacular land exists in the whole world, no more stirring histories are as concentrated in any one region as in the state of Rajasthan, erstwhile Rajputana. Rajasthan, where mountains have been thrown up from the burning sands of the desert, where legends have created lakes and pools, where a proud and mysterious people have built forts and palaces, temples and mansions. Here, where kingdoms once fought over codes of honour and chivalry rather than wealth and power, families still feud long after the last battle has been consigned to the pages of history.

But history has not been forgotten. There were twenty-two kingdoms that formed Rajputana once, which in their misfortunes and those of the nobility have left some branches of the families destitute, while others still live, like the Thakurs, the Rawals and the maharajas. In 1947, India gained independence, but the twenty-two families who merged to form the state of Rajasthan in the Union of India gave up their independence. A few decades later they also lost their privileges. A whole era of pomp and pageantry, celebration and patronage had come to pass.

But the princes have not gone. They still inhabit a land where a centuries-old history has not been forgotten. Blue blood recognises its own, and though there might be bitterness still over slights and battles generations old, the princes group together during rituals, ceremonies and durbars.

Though mere ceremonies bereft of meaning in modern, democratic India, the spirit behind them has withstood the test of centuries. And for these royal families, reduced to an ordinariness almost overnight, they are an affirmation of a past that was once the destiny of their ancestors.

Despite decades of new lifestyles, it is impossible for them to move away from a princely past. They reside in stately palaces that make their European counterparts look dowdy and miniscule in comparison, their heritage is on display in forts that are now repositories of their historic treasures. Their grand wealth, locked away in vaults, is aired annually and still draws gasps of wonder. Though they now preside over corporate durbars, but the homage of the people is still their due. Their coat of arms and their emblems sit proudly on the grills of cars and gates and on the flags that flutter atop their sprawling residences. The muzzle of the gun on *shikaar* expeditions has been replaced by that of the camera during safaris.

Theirs was not an ordinary life. At times it read like a fairy tale. But then, this is how it is with any resident of the desert who has to till the soil to eke out a livelihood that is still dependent on an infrequent visitor, Indra, the Lord of Rain. Maharajas once painted apartments with rain clouds so that in years of drought these could provide the solace of remembered relief.

If the rains were alien to many a villager, the gods, in fact, were less alien. For the proud warrior race of the Rajputs has always laid claim to descend from the gods, with the sun, the moon and the sacred fire as their progenitors. These led

to the classifications of the clans as the sun-born Suryavanshis, the moon-begotten Chandravanshis, and the fire-born Agnikuls. They trace their origin, to Lord Rama and to Lord Krishna. Fanciful though the claim may be, that inevitable chronicler of Rajput fortunes, Colonel James Tod, who toured these kingdoms during the British presence in India, has recorded: 'If we compare the antiquity and illustrious descent of dynasties which have ruled the small sovereignties of Rajasthan, with many a celebrity in Europe, superiority will often attach to the Rajput. From the most remote periods we can trace nothing ignoble, nor any vestige of vassal origin. Reduced in power, circumcised in territory, compelled to yield much of their splendour and many of the dignities of birth, they have not abandoned an iota of the pride and high bearing arising from a knowledge of their illustrious and regal descent.'

Over a century and a half later, Bapji, the Maharaja of Jodhpur, or Maharaja Gaj Singh II of Marwar, confirms, 'I am proud of my ancestors.' According to him, 'My ancestors ruled in such a manner that people felt they were a part of that society; they knew there

was justice; decisions were taken according to a process. It may not have been a sophisticated legal process, but at least it was not a delayed legal process.'

The people turned inevitably to their ruling family for anything they required. Colonel Tod wrote in 1829: 'The poorest Rajput to this day retains all the pride of ancestry, often his sole inheritance...' A shared history, and the participative 'genius of these Rajput princes, as statesmen and warriors' has created a bond that time and the changing circumstances have not been able to sunder.

And so, in northwestern India, and part of the great Thar desert, in a state bigger than Belgium and Holland combined, people still colour the arid landscape with tales of their past. In countless fairs, in dusty villages, in distinctive princely kingdoms, through bard and lore, through magnificent citadels and painted homes, the spirit of Rajasthan endures.

Home of the peacock in all its splendour, of stirring ballads, of the tiger in lush jungles, and of delicate palaces set afloat on picturesque blue lakes, Rajasthan is a study in contrasts, a changing kaleidoscope of images, where forts and fortunes held the key to not just the states of the desert, but to all of India.

Once upon a time was just a little while ago. For, as Rudyard Kipling wrote, 'If any part of a land is strewn with dead men's bones Rajputana has a special claim to distinction.'

A painted wall in Shekhawati. Some of the finest frescos can be found on the walls of mansions owned by Marwari traders. Cavalries comprising elephants, horses and camels were particular favourites as were processions, and these incorporated complete walls as their canvas.

5

Preceding pages 6-7: Jaipur is watched over by three forts: its former capital, Amber; the seat of the Kachchwaha treasury, Jaigarh; and Nahargarh, the summer retreat for the zenana or women's wing of the palace. Built in 1734 to protect Jai Singh's new city, Nahargarh provides spectacular views from its ramparts, particularly at sunset. Its elaborate apartments were added by Ram Singh in 1868. *Preceding pages 8-9:* The Aravalli hills that had provided protection to Chittaurgarh became a decorative feature ringing Udai Singh's new city, Udaipur. Covering an island in Lake Pichola, the Lake Palace appears to be afloat. The romantic 18th century summer palace faces the more formidable City Palace (foreground) with its stark, sheer walls that end in a cornucopia of decorative arches, domes and turrets. *Preceding pages 10-11:* The Shekhawati region of Rajasthan forms a triangular pocket between Jaipur, Bikaner and Delhi, and has been the state of origin of many of India's leading financial and industrial families. The ancestral homes of these traders are called havelis, which were profusely painted by local artists in the fresco bueno style. Here a detail of a fresco from a jeweller's showroom, Sone Chandi ki Dukan, in the town of Mahansar.

This page: *In Samode Palace, dancers enact one of Rajasthan's many dance forms. The rawals, titular chiefs of Samode, served as prime ministers in the court of Jaipur. It is believed that when the rawal of Samode chanced upon a hill close to Jaipur, he first built his palace here, and then informed the Jaipur Maharaja, lest the ruler utilise the site for himself. Samode Palace is currently a heritage hotel where guests can stay.*

Following pages 14-15: *Rajasthan once consisted of 22 independent kingdoms. At the time of India's independence, these kingdoms merged with the Indian Union, and the royal families were extended certain privileges in return. The government later withdrew these, and the royals have since had to fend for themselves. While a few families have found it hard to survive, Maharaja Gaj Singh II of Jodhpur (here, with his family) has turned his heritage into an asset.*

Following pages 16-17: *As Jaisalmer grew, people established homes outside its fortifications, but once the entire community used to live within this 12th century fort established by the Bhatti descendants of Lord Krishna. The clan was driven to the desert because it could rarely restrain itself from pillaging caravans of goods.* **Following pages 18-19:** *Pushkar, a place of Hindu pilgrimage near Ajmer, comes into focus during its annual mela or fair. The religious come to bathe on the full moon night in the holy water tank of the only Brahma temple, but the main purpose is a vast camp set up for the trading of horses, camels and cattle. For a week, Pushkar becomes a unique theatre of the colourful Rajasthani way of life.*

13

Jaipur has been called India's pink city, an euphemism that is misplaced, for the walls of the capital of Rajasthan and one of its greatest kingdoms are a soft orange, or a burnt peach. The city, ringed by hills where once the maharajas went on *shikaar,* are still forested and green, but Jaipur is today a modern city. Its industry is handicrafts. Everywhere one finds jewellers, handblock printers, marble and bangles makers producing exquisite handicrafts.

Jaipur is a handsome town, and in one of its many palaces lives the legendary beauty, Rajmata

Gayatri Devi, the queen mother, who decades ago was voted one of the world's most beautiful women. With the same graciousness with which she accepted the task of hostess as Maharaja Man Singh's third bride, she today runs schools and supervises a stud farm. In another palace at the heart of the city lives her stepson and Jaipur's maharaja, Brigadier Sawai Bhawani Singh, fondly nicknamed 'Bubbles' by a nanny who was struck by the amount of champagne that flowed on his birth. Sundry other palaces are occupied by other members of the family, while many buildings have been converted into luxurious palace hotels.

Jaipur is glamorous. But long before there was a Jaipur, its rulers occupied the hill

fortress of Amber, named after Ambikeshwara, a temple dedicated to Lord Shiva.

It was to this destination that a scion of the house of Narwar journeyed from Dausa, where he was camping, a short journey that entailed marrying into the family that held the fort, and then betraying its trust to wrest control of this powerful and rich region. On this deed rests the foundation of a kingdom that lasted for eight centuries, the last two of which saw the shifting of the capital to nearby Jaipur.

Like the rest of the princely states, Amber's (and later Jaipur's) might was formidable, its rulers men of imagination and awesome power. But when the Mughals occupied Agra, and then Delhi, Amber chose to befriend its foes. This it did by offering in marriage one of the daughters of the royal house to Akbar, the Mughal emperor. This alliance paved the way for a mutual friendship that enhanced Amber's fortunes. Its revenues increased, its status as an imperial ally went up and a period of comparative peace followed.

Of course, Amber's armies were often put at the disposal of its imperial rulers, employed in Bengal in the east and the Deccan in the south. These military campaigns, many of them under the generalship of Maharaja Man Singh, won even greater favours. And when the young Maharaja Jai Singh impressed the ageing Shahenshah Aurangzeb with his ready wit, the house of Amber earned itself the title of *Sawai* (literally, one and a quarter), placing it above the other princes.

Having proved his mettle and having, in turn, been characterised by it, Maharaja Jai Singh took the momentous decision of shifting his capital from Amber. He chose a site in the valley below the

Amber sprawls atop Kalikhoh Hill, the first capital of the Kachchwahas after they had been routed from Narwar (near Gwalior). The fort, added by generations of rulers, has a distinctive style of architecture that was later emulated in the building of Jaipur.

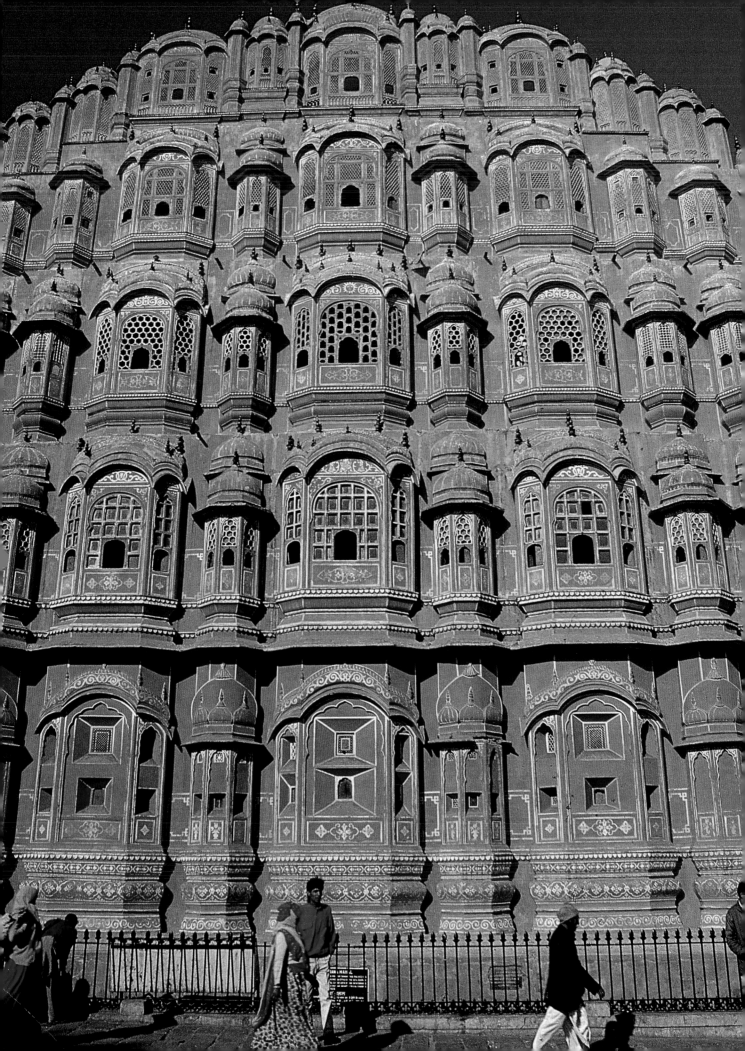

hills of Amber, and named it Jaipur (the city of victory but also his own name).

Amber had been built over centuries by succeeding rulers. Jai Singh wanted his new city to be one of a kind and modern. In his endeavour to plan such a city he employed Vidyadhar, a Bengali Brahmin, who laid the foundations of the capital acording to the ancient Indian treatise on architecture. The straight roads were lined with buildings, the plans for each of which were personally approved by Vidyadhar. The city was planned in seven squares. At its heart was the City Palace complex with its seven-tiered Chandra Mahal where the present maharaja still resides. The complex also catered to another of the ruler's passions, astronomy, with the construction of the Jantar Mantar, the world's largest open-air astronomical laboratory, from where Jaipur time was strictly maintained.

Close to the City Palace are the Ram Niwas Public Gardens laid by Maharaja Ram Singh who in the mid-19th century gave Jaipur many of its modern conveniences, like gas lighting on the streets, or a theatre, and who proved to be an amateur photographer of class. Within these gardens is Albert Hall, a museum that was conceived by an English architect, Sir Swinton Jacob, who was strongly influenced by Rajput architecture.

On the outskirts of town, two pleasure gardens, Vidyadharji ka Bagh, and Sisodia Rani ka Bagh, continue to be wonderful summer retreats with one essential difference—they are now open to the public.

Jaipur's signature building, however, is Hawa Mahal (palace of breezes), a marvel of construction five storeys high and with 953 windows, built within the City Palace complex by Maharaja Pratap Singh in the late 18th century. Its purpose was imaginative. Seated behind its windows, women of the royal household could look out on to Jaipur and observe state processions, without being themselves seen.

Though Amber was Jaipur's original capital, it was not its only fort, for close by, cresting the same range of the Aravallis, are two other forts, Nahargarh and Jaigarh. Jaigarh was planned about the same time that the foundation of Jaipur was being laid. The centre of the state's gun foundry, tales of the fabulous treasures hidden here abound. For centuries this had been the repository of the

Above: The large silver urns were filled with Ganga water for Maharaja Madho Singh's maiden journey to London. The urns are listed in the Guiness Book as the largest silver objects in the world. ***Below:*** Rajmata Gayatri Devi stands in the City Palace complex of Jaipur. The City Palace is home to her stepson, the maharaja, and is run by a trust as a museum. ***Facing page:*** Hawa Mahal, part of the City Palace complex, overlooks the streets of the busy bazaar. Its purpose was to allow the women of the royal household to observe processions without the violation of their privacy.

Top: *Dancers against the backdrop of Tripolia Gate, Jaipur, during one of the city's many festive occasions.*
Middle: *A silver doorway within a painted arch in Pritam Chowk, part of the Jaipur City Palace complex.*
Bottom: *Jaivana, believed to be the largest cannon on wheels in the world, stands sentinel over the ramparts of Jaigarh which served as the kingdom's gun foundry.*
Facing page: *Ganesh Pol in Amber forms the gateway to the private apartments of the maharaja, and the zenana deodi or women's palace.*

Jaipur treasury, and it is believed that Mina tribesmen used to guard this wealth with their life. Just once, in the year of their succession to the throne, Jaipur's maharajas were led blindfolded to this treasure and allowed to pick any one object that caught their fancy. Whether this story is indeed true has never been ascertained, and the present head of the family maintains a tight-lipped silence on it. However, when income tax authorities decided to verify the rumours, they found nothing, leading to speculation that the treasure had been removed prior to the raid.

Jaipur, like any other city, has grown far beyond the limits set by its founder, and its hunting lodges, such as Rambagh, have now been absorbed into the city. Rambagh, in fact, was later converted into the official residence of Maharaja Man Singh II and Gayatri Devi and is now a vintage hotel.

Several other palaces and stately homes have since been converted into hotels. These include Raj Mahal and Jai Mahal, while stately homes of the aristocracy too have been witness to a similar reconversion, including the townhouses of the families of Khetri, Mandawa and Bissau, once important Shekhawati fiefdoms.

But 40 kms out of Jaipur is Samode, one of Jaipur's most brilliant heritage hotels. Samode was an important *thikana* (feudatory state) of Jaipur, and along with Chomu, was one of its principal kingmakers. Chomu erred in opposing the adoption of Maharaja Man Singh to the Jaipur *gaddi* and suffered for it. So much so that Rajmata Gayatri Devi still refuses to take the name of the *thikana* that opposed her husband's succession to the throne.

Samode *rawals* were prime ministers to the court of Jaipur, and their fortune was converted into a palatial residence with sumptuous decorated apartments. Painted in the neighbouring Shekhawati style, Samode was converted into a hotel by the two brothers who succeeded to their father's title, and who were able to convert a family liability into an asset.

Samode's Durbar Hall is without doubt sumptuous. It is lavishly painted, with red and gold dominating the walls and a chandelier suspended from a high ceiling. Balconies with windows overlook the room, from where queens and princes would observe the proceedings of state. The courtyards and rooms of the aristocratic family are now open to guests.

The durbar hall at Samode Palace near Jaipur is profusely painted with frescos, and provides a grand setting for entertainments.

Castle Mandawa is a typical example of the fortified settlements dotting the Shekhawati region, from where the thakurs or feudatory chiefs commanded their independent armies. The chiefs owed allegiance to the house of Jaipur, but for many decades refused to recognise its status. However, inheritance by primogeniture led to internecine battles and so the Shekhawati was never able to consolidate itself into a single kingdom.

The region north of Jaipur lying trapped between Bikaner and Delhi is called the **Shekhawati.** This is a loosely held confederation of a large number of towns that were once ruled by different members of the Shekhawat family. This arid part of the desert has given rise to the largest number of trading families called Marwaris, now settled all over the country and controlling the financial interests of the nation. Though most of them no longer live in the towns of Shekhawati, their ancestral homes provide the richest concentration of frescos seen anywhere in the world.

What is now still known as the Shekhawati region was once held as small fiefdoms by the Kayamkhani nawabs and a few Rajput families. A small principality in this area, Barwada, was held by a cousin of the house of Amber. But Mokul Singh—for that was his name—who ruled from 1430-45, found himself bereft of an heir despite three marriages. In order to please the gods, he went on a pilgrimage to Brindavan, the holy area near Agra which is closely associated with Lord Krishna, the dark-skinned, playful hero-god of the Indian epics.

In Brindavan, a spiritual mentor blessed Mokul with a son. He was sent back to Barwada with an idol of Krishna, and instructed to graze cows. Abandoning his administrative duties, Mokul proceeded to abide by his guru's decree, and in the fields chanced upon another holy man, a Muslim, Sheikh Burhan. The sheikh too prophesied a son for Mokul Singh, and predicted a golden future for him provided the newly born was bathed in the blood of a freshly sacrificed calf.

In 1433 this son was born to Mokul. He was named Shekha. Brindavan's Krishna and the Muslim fakir's blue cloth have since become standard pennants in the region. As a Hindu, the royal

baby was bathed not in calf's but in goat's blood. But despite that, Shekha went on to establish a dynasty that still continues to reside in the towns of Shekhawati, and in Jaipur.

Shekha declared war on Amber by refusing to send the customary colt as a token of allegiance, and won to become an independent ruler. He also built forts and extended his territories. Under his rule, the region became known as the Garden of Shekha (Shekhawati).

His sons and grandsons extended the might of Shekhawati, and their ongoing aggressions against Amber caused their cousins sleepless nights. Eight generations after Shekha, Shardul Singh was able to oust the Kayamkhanis from the region, making the Shekhawat Rajput's rule supreme.

However, though the inheritance procedure of the Shekhawats was based on primogeniture, each son was given equal share in his father's territories. This meant that not only was Shekhawati unable to consolidate as one kingdom, but progressive growth meant the Shekhawats involving themselves in a great deal of infighting. Eventually, therefore, Maharaja Jai Singh, who had shifted his capital

While the Rajput chiefs provided protection, the Marwari trading families controlled vast wealth earned through a system of trading which they controlled via the caravan routes that passed through Shekhawati. Merchants here could set rates for goods in distant Burma. With this wealth, they built themselves sprawling havelis which were adorned with frescos, and their philanthropic pursuits included the building of wells, temples and dharamshalas.

from Amber to Jaipur, was able once again to assert his suzerainty over them.

Since Shekhawati lay along the overland trade routes, it was a lucrative area for the merchants or Marwaris, who lived here. They served the Rajput kings and went on military campaigns with them to the east and the south. Later, with the British hoping to build bridges with the local communities to source raw materials, the Marwaris came to serve in British-held towns.

These wealthy Marwaris built massive mansions called *havelis*. Impressive in size, over time these *havelis* came to be profusely painted with frescos depicting gods and kings, flowers and arabesques

Top: *The Rathore Rajputs of Marwar established kingdoms beyond Jodhpur. One of these was Kishangarh known for the exquisite quality of miniature paintings.* ***Middle:*** *Kotah was carved out of its parent state, Bundi, and went on to become the larger Hada kingdom. Both have fortified palaces and exquisite painted apartments.* ***Bottom:*** *Alwar was created as a state in the 18th century out of Jaipur. It became one of four princely kingdoms (the other three being Bharatpur, Dholpur and Karoli) that got together to form an independent United States of Matsya. In 1947 they merged with the state of Rajasthan.*

and scenes from everyday life. Depictions of colonial life and inventions added a touch of humour.

But then, the leading families too moved away from Shekhawati, to settle in Calcutta, Bombay, Surat and Hyderabad, and the Shekhawati towns— Bissau, Dundlod, Fatehpur, Jhunjhunu, Khetri, Lakshmangarh, Mahansar, Mandawa, Mukundgarh, Nawalgarh, Parasrampura, Ramgarh, Ratangarh, Sikar, Singhana—were abandoned. It is only in the last two decades that the Shekhawati region has acquired a fillip, with its art being the central focus. And the children of the house of Shekha, most of whom too had abandoned their family castles to settle in Jaipur, are now back, opening dusty palaces and converting them into hotels.

Kishangarh is named as much after Krishna as its founder, Kishan Singh, who claimed his right to the kingdom in 1611. Kishangarh was a small kingdom close to Ajmer. Its fortunes have seen battles and sieges, but its most significant contribution has been to Indian art. For the ateliers of Kishangarh produced brilliant miniature paintings the likes of which are not seen anywhere in Rajasthan. One of the greatest patrons of art, Raja Satwant Singh, based a portrait of Krishna's consort, Radha, on his own mistress, Bani Thani. The long aquiline nose, and the elongated eyes are a hallmark of the Rajput woman's beauty. Satwant Singh eventually abandoned his court, and left with his mistress for Brindavan.

Another road out of Jaipur leads to **Tonk,** once the state's only Muslim kingdom and today known for its Sunehri Kothi or golden palace. The road ends in the twin kingdoms of Bundi and Kotah, Hada kingdoms claiming descent from fire.

A Hada chief, Rao Deva Singh, captured **Bundi** from a Mina tribe in 1241 and laid the foundation of an empire. Entrenched in a rugged hill, Bundi is crowned by Taragarh, a huge, impressive fort. At the base of Taragarh sits one of the finest examples of Rajput architecture, Bundi Palace.

Bundi too is known for its excellent paintings, and the Chitrashala or hall of paintings has some of the best known works seen in any Rajasthani palace. Rudyard Kipling, the writer, stayed at Bundi. Initially unhappy about his welcome to Bundi, he was housed in a pavilion 'open to the winds of heaven, and the pigeons of the Raja'. But the latter had 'polluted more than the first could purify', and Kipling found that it was, in fact, 'a

*Top: Wrested in the 13th century from the Minas by the Hada Rajputs, Bundi's Taragarh Fort is one of the finest examples of Rajput architecture. In the 18th century, Umed Singh commissioned its Chitrashala, an art gallery with scenes depicting the Ras Leela and court life. **Middle:** The merchants of Shekhawati not only painted their havelis, the inside chambers were decorated with the use of inlay, glass and mirrors. Here, the ceiling of the Chaudhari haveli in Fatehpur. **Bottom:** Sunehri Kothi, the golden palace of Tonk, in all its splendour. Tonk was the only Muslim kingdom of Rajasthan.*

beautifully lazy city, doing everything in the real, true, original native way…'

Kotah was a *jagir* of the eldest prince of Bundi. Founded in 1264, a few years later than Bundi, it became independent in 1624 when Madho Singh, the second son of Rattan Singh of Bundi, was made its ruler by the Mughal emperor, Aurangzeb.

Like Bundi, the artists of Kotah were celebrated, and the fortified City Palace is replete with wall paintings depicting scenes of battle and the hunt. While the head of Bundi shuns publicity, Maharao Brijraj Singh of Kotah has turned to scholarship. Both family palaces have been turned into hotels.

Alwar has not been as lucky. Located on the old highway between Jaipur and Delhi, its vast palaces have been locked because of legal disputes. It has now been bypassed for its more popular hunting lodge in Sariska, a protected tiger reserve. Once a Mewat kingdom, it was carved into an independent state in the 18th century by the shrewd maneouvrings of a distant relative of the Jaipur family, Thakur Pratap Singh. He manipulated recognition from the Mughals and consolidated his gains. The British, then emerging as a power, sought his assistance and declared him maharaja. Alwar thus became a kingdom.

The City Palace 'recalls the dreams of magnificence', even though it is now the seat of the provincial bureaucracy. There is also Bala Kila, the original fort which was wrested from the Jats by Pratap Singh in 1775. But the *coup de grace* of Alwar is its huge Vijay Mandir Palace, set by the side of a lake, built by the eccentric Maharaja Jai Singh in the early 20th century. A museum in the City Palace houses some magnificent royal artifacts.

Bikaner was founded in 1486 by the scion of this Rathore stronghold. The city of Jodhpur had just been founded, and Rao Jodha sat on the *gaddi* of one of Rajputana's most powerful states.

Since rulers carried with them the weight of not only governance but also a zealous guard against intrigue, it is possible that Rao Jodha misunderstood a whisper between his brother, Kandal, and second son, Bika. 'Are you planning the conquest of an empire?' he asked them in full court. They took great offence to this. Kandal, Bika and a group of retainers left the court of Jodhpur in search of their own fortunes.

After various victories they came upon a woman revered as a living saint, Karni Mata. She blessed them, prophesying that Bika's empire would one

31

day extend beyond that of his father. Near Karni Mata's sanctuary, Bikaner was established. It lived up to its prophesy, but Jodhpur and Bikaner remained in conflict thereafter. Part of the bitterness set in when Bika claimed the symbols and the *pugal*, the throne of Marwar that the family had carried with it from its original capital, Kanauj.

Bikaner's principal fort, Junagarh, was founded by Raja Rai Singh, an ally of the Mughal king, Akbar. Cementing the bond further was Prithviraj Singh, or Peethal, one of the 'nine gems' of the Mughal court, who remained a loyal Rajput. It so happened that the *rana* of Chittaur, Pratap sent a message of surrender to Akbar. Chittaur was a symbol of Rajput pride, and Peethal claimed the missive to be a forgery. He wrote in stirring verse to the *rana* of how his moustache would hang limp in shame should the latter indeed surrender. This enthused the *rana* so much that the surrender never took place.

Various rulers added to Bikaner's influence but undoubtedly it was Maharaja Ganga Singh whose contribution was the greatest. He became the ruler of Bikaner at the end of the 19th century, and died shortly before the independence of India. In this period, he was able to give Bikaner a modern palace, educational institutions, a railway network and bring the waters of a river to the desert. Much of this was achieved through wildly successful *shikaar* expeditions with British rulers.

His grandson, Karni Singh, a painter, scholar and marksman of repute, represented and gained several golds in the olympics. The former home of Ganga Singh is now a hotel, though part of it is still a royal residence.

Bharatpur is today known as the country's finest bird sanctuary, but before independence its fame was more generic. Bharatpur was the premier Jat state in Rajasthan, Dholpur being the other one.

In a sense Bharatpur is the legacy of Churaman, a Jat overlord whose forces were a source of constant irritation to the Mughals in the late 17th century. The Mughals retaliated by destroying Jat villages. The Jats later regrouped under Badan Singh who firmly entrenched himself in a belt along the river Jamuna between Delhi and Agra.

Badan Singh established and founded the fort and palaces of Deeg in 1725. Seven years later, his son laid the foundation nearby of the fort of Bharatpur. It was a formidable structure called Lohagarh (iron fort), which lived up to its

*Soon after the founding of Jodhpur, a scion of the house established the kingdom of Bikaner. At its heart lay Junagarh Fort. Within its battlements, rulers raised some of the most marvellous palaces, such as the throne rooms of Anup Mahal **(top and bottom)** and Karan Mahal **(middle)**. The walls of the rooms were polished alabaster, but have withstood the ravages of centuries.*
***Facing page:** The Lallgarh Band practices in Junagarh Fort. The pierced sandstone staircase is a turn-of-the-century addition to the fort made by Bikaner's most progressive ruler, Maharaja Ganga Singh.*

33

reputation. On several occasion the British laid siege to it but were unable to take it.

The fort was made impregnable through the simple device of surrounding it with massive earth walls and a moat. Missiles aimed at the fort were absorbed by the mud walls and failed to have any impact. The former royal family is in residence in a modern palace. However, it is Deeg which is a showcase of Jat architecture. Several war trophies including a marble swing that belonged to Shah Jehan can be seen here.

Dholpur was granted as a state to the Jats in 1805 from the original kingdom of Gohad. Close to Gwalior, Dholpur's rocky landscape is famous for its red sandstone. The Chambal river here was often the geographical dividing line between Rajputana and the Maratha kingdoms.

The kingdom of **Karauli** was once known for its tiger *shikaar* and retained trained cheetahs in court. The Jadon Rajput kings were followers of Krishna, and renowned for their delicate architecture. The City Palace complex has been badly desecrated. But the grandeur of the structure, the elegance of fluted pillars and the majesty of the gateways is still in evidence.

Above: In Bharatpur, a magnificent 20th century palace is the residence of a prince who is interested in political and social work. The fort of Bharatpur was made impregnable by mud walls which absorbed the impact of missiles. Today, Bharatpur is better known for its bird sanctuary, formed by a maharaja who flooded the area and used it for duck shoots. **Facing page:** The head of the Karauli family strolls through the ruins of the kingdom's former capital. Heads of ruling families still command respect, though they have little to offer their people apart from their lineage, and a history of loyalty. **Following pages 36-37:** It is believed that the holy sarovar or pond of Pushkar was formed when Brahma dropped the petals of a lotus here. Ancient belief has bestowed these waters with healing power but according to legend the gods were worried when they saw large numbers of people who would come asking for a boon from Brahma. As a result, Brahma cut short the period of boon to three days in a year, which is when the annual Pushkar fair is held.

You will encounter more people at **Pushkar** than almost anywhere else in Rajasthan during the annual week-long fair that takes place here in November, during the period of the full moon, and during Kartik Purnima. And yet, Pushkar is but a small place, and the fair one of countless held in the state.

Aeons ago, or so it is said, the petals of Brahma's lotus floated to earth and fell on Pushkar. As a result a lake sprang up here, and the gods decided to hold a sacrificial fire to cleanse the whole world. Proceedings for the ritual went apace, but Brahma's wife, a habitual latecomer, found upon her arrival that her spouse had gone ahead with the ceremonies, replacing her with a milkmaid. Enraged, she cursed Brahma, saying he would henceforth be worshipped on earth at only one place, Pushkar, and departed.

And Brahma indeed is worshipped only at Pushkar, in a solitary temple, while the other two gods of the trinity, Vishnu and Shiva, have millions of temples consecrated in their honour all over the country.

But Brahma's devotees more than make up for it during Kartik Purnima, when they journey from all over Rajasthan, and from the neighbouring states to set up camp here. They bathe in the holy lake by moonlight as they believe this cures all diseases.

Pushkar is ideal for observing faces. Garbed in their festive best, the men rival the women, in their colourful turbans, ears, neck and ankles festooned with jewellery, and the body sporting tattoos.

The largest camel trading fair in the country takes place simultaneously at Pushkar. Of course, horses are bought and sold too, and so are donkeys. And a colourful village bazaar becomes a meeting ground for trading in handicrafts on the one hand and goods from cities on the other. Families meet, gossip, and arrange matrimonial alliances. There are campfires with haunting wisps of smoke, and of couse, there is music and dancing.

But most of all, there are the people at Pushkar, strikingly good-looking women and handsome men in their colourful dresses, spread out much like a rainbow upon the blond sands of an ancient land.

Visitors to Pushkar can find accommodation in a tented city close to the holy city of Ajmer, where the Mughal emperors once came to pay homage at the dargah. After the mela or fair, the tents, like the people, disappear, but come November and the annual rendezvous, they'll all be back, and the enchantment will begin all over again...

Following pages 40-41: *A golden baze of sand envelops the stark landscape around Pushkar in November. People from far have gathered here, journeying on foot, by bus, in tractor trolleys. Here they will pray to Brahma, catch up on gossip, and buy and sell animals, horses and cattle. But Pushkar is not a tedium; it is an annual event Rajasthan looks forward to.*

Top: *Umaid Bhawan Palace is currently a hotel and the royal residence. The chief intention of the architect appears to have been a building that would rival the splendour of the Viceregal Lodge in New Delhi, then under construction.* ***Middle:*** *Meherangarh Fort rises magnificently from the steep hill it crowns, making it impossible to scale. Even when it was built, the fortifications were high and rugged, and crowning the bastions were the royal apartments.* ***Bottom:*** *All Jodhpur rulers had chhatris or memorial cenotaphs at Mandore, the old capital, but Maharaja Jaswant Singh's chhatri at Jaswant Thada, built in 1899 in marble and exquisitely carved, is located to one side of Meherangarh.*

The Maharaja of Karauli lives in Jaipur, but the palace of his former kingdom is still his home. Here he grows crops, and lives in splendour but as an occasional visitor. The rooms of the palace, designed by his grandfather, are spacious, and are now let out to guests. His garages hold vintage cars, and he has horses for riding. And as he saunters through the grounds, retainers bow deep in obeisance. In these brief moments he is still a maharaja, and reality is a fleeting lie.

Jodhpur finds it difficult to come to terms with the present simply because its symbols are all irresistibly of the past. A huge fort, Meherangarh, sentinel of the Marwar empire and the key to Rathore's invincibility, grows out of the rocky outcrops of a huge hill. On another, lower hill, is a striking palace, with dome and turrets more European than Rajput, but nonetheless impressive. And in between, a bustling city where wood furniture is lacquered, women deftly tie and dye yards of fabric, where a cobbler embroiders motifs with coloured yarn on *jutees,* the sturdy slip-on shoes sported by the people of the desert.

Without doubt Jodhpur is a city of the past. True, ancient palaces may have become hotels, but the dust still flies from the horses' hooves as opponents settle scores over polo jousts. And when the maharaja has his birthday, the nobles of the state turn up at his imposing palace to re-enact a ceremony of homage and support that traces its origins back to Kanauj and to the dawn of this kingdom.

The Rathore rulers were kings at Kanauj, an empire close to modern-day Kanpur in Uttar Pradesh, which they won and occupied from 470 to 1193, until it was sacked by Mohammad Ghori. Raja Jai Chand then moved out with the remnants of his vassalage, but dispirited by the defeat, he drowned while crossing the Ganga. His heir, Sheoji, and a mere handful of people, set themselves up at Pali, near today's Jodhpur.

Needless to say, battles followed, and many of the intrigues were between this newly-founded kingdom and Mewar (today, Udaipur). The capital was shifted from Pali to Mandore, and then finally in 1459, to Jodhpur, which was named after Rao Jodha who had laid the foundation of its massive fort on the advice of a holy man who had suggested a hilltop fort.

From the ramparts of Meherangarh (then called Jodhagarh), the land of the Rathores spread all

around, and on a clear day, the towers of warring Kumbhalgarh could be seen. Towers were built from where endless vigil was kept. When completed, and in keeping with tradition, their architect was thrown into its foundations, its defence secrets intact.

Only a few years were to pass before the son of Jodha, Bika, rode out to establish his own empire, Bikaner. Thereafter Jodhpur and Bikaner clashed on many occasions.

Raja Udai Singh won peace with the Mughals. He was succeeded by Jaswant Singh, who was crowned maharaja. His constant alignment, now with Shah Jehan and then with rebellious Aurangzeb, cost him dear. He enraged a newly anointed Aurangzeb, who defeated Jaswant Singh's army. When the ruler returned to Meherangarh, an angry queen told him that a Rajput should die on the battlefield rather then return defeated. Jaswant Singh went on to die in the battlefield, and his queens immolated themselves by fire in the *jauhar* ceremony.

But Jaswant Singh's infant son, Ajit Singh, was rescued by one of Rajputana's greatest heroes, Durga Das. While Aurangzeb's forces sacked Marwar, Durga Das fled with the child to the mountains, and brought him up there in the tradition befitting a future ruler. Thirty years later, Durga Das and Ajit Singh stormed the Mughal forces and claimed their right.

Relationships with the British were more cordial. A time was to come when Sir Pratap was to tick off the Prince of Wales, later King George V, for dismounting while pig sticking, in the following words: 'I know you Prince of Wales, you know you Prince of Wales, but pig no know you Prince of Wales!' The famous Jodhpur breeches were designed by him.

Maharaja Umaid Singh, however, was a modern prince and felt the need for building a contemporary residence for himself. However, it was a famine that actually spurred the construction, and in 1929, atop Chhattar Hill, Umaid Bhawan

Top and middle: Phool Mahal in Meherangarh is richly gilded and exquisite in its details. The intricate arches are enhanced by delicate scalloping and the royal colours, yellow and red, still dominate. ***Bottom:*** A section of the fort has been turned into a museum, and from the throne to bristling weaponry, the might of the warrior princes is on proud display.

was laid out. Its architect was Sir Herbert Lanchester who had hoped to design New Delhi, British India's emerging and powerful capital.

So it was that for sixteen years, three thousand labourers struggled to create a 347-room palace that, though looking dazzlingly English, is in fact suitable for a Rajput potentate's residence. The swimming pool was placed indoors, complete with signs of the zodiac. It had its own private auditorium, eight kitchens and a ballroom to seat three hundred. A double dome topped the centre of the mammoth building that measured 195 metres by 103 metres. A passing Polish painter, Norblin, did the murals for the suites. Furniture was ordered twice from a factory in Britain, but war ensured that the first consignment was bombed at sea, while in the second instance the factory itself was razed to the ground. Eventually, the art nouveau designs were simply copied by local carpenters.

Jaisalmer is known for its *havelis*, built on a massive scale, for the residences of merchants that allowed women access to the world outside only through the windows and pierced stone screens. In Jaisalmer, the merchants had acquired a role akin to kingship, and their residences were all the more opulent. In fact, Salim Singh, one of the kingdom's most important traders, and *diwan* of the state, harboured ambitions similar to those of the Maharawal (as the ruler of Jaisalmer is addressed).

Salim Singh's father was a powerful prime minister in the court of the Maharawal. Jaisalmer, being a trading outpost, was immensely rich, its court rife with intrigue. Salim's father was murdered in one such intriguing incident. Salim swore revenge and with great dexterity got rid of several courtiers and princes. By the time he came of age, he was so powerful that the ruler, Maharawal Mool Raj, had no choice but to appoint him *diwan*.

As the state's prime minister, Salim Singh commissioned his impressive 18th century *haveli*. When completed, it was topped by blue cupolas, the upper storey supported on carved brackets. Into this imposing residence Salim Singh moved with his seven wives and two concubines. He then decided to build a bridge from his *haveli* to the Maharawal's palace. This, however, Mool Raj opposed, fearing for his own safety. And while Salim Singh plotted in his haveli, his evil machinations culminated in his own murder.

Other *havelis*, however, were built with

Above: *Nathmalji ki Haveli was one of the city's last great havelis to be commissioned, and was ordered by the ruler for his prime minister.* ***Below:*** *Close up of the pierced sandstone windows of Patwon ki Haveli.*
Preceding pages 44-45: *Village women gather in one of the principal courtyards of Meherangarh Fort where maharajas were anointed as heads of the family. Buff sandstone has been used for most of the construction, because it blended with the natural colour of the hill, and was adequate for carving. The stone pierced window screens allowed the women of the zenana to look out over the courtyard and witness important ceremonies, and also acted as a sun-shield.* ***Facing page:*** *Facade of the pierced stone windows of Patwon ki Haveli in Jaisalmer, its two sides carved by two Muslim brothers.*

seemingly less evil intent. Easily the most impressive is Patwon ki Haveli, a group of five residences planned in a *cul de sac*. Patwas were traders and made their money as moneylenders and opium smugglers. Their riches were converted into five linked residences, every part profusely carved and decorated with friezes and screens. Built between 1800-60, the *havelis,* like the others in Jaisalmer, were made of yellow sandstone. The carvings were inspired by Rajput and Islamic traditions.

The last of Jaisalmer's great mansions is Nathmalji ki Haveli. Mohata Nathmal too was a *diwan* in the state, and so respected was he that Maharawal Beri Saal had the delicately carved yellow sandstone building specially commissioned for him.

The *silvataa* community of stone carvers then set about to create a palace for the Maharawal, but though it was ostentatiously carved in the same yellow sandstone, it was not able to achieve the perfection of the merchants' *havelis.*

The decline in Jaisalmer's fortunes set in during the 20th century, with the ports of Calcutta and Bombay now controlling sea trades, while overland trading routes declined. Jaisalmer got isolated. And the desert once again ruled supreme.

The Bhatti Rajputs and the nomads defy the dry and difficult desert with their traditions and their lifestyle. They cover their homes with a coating of clay and cowdung to keep them cool and make them antiseptic. On these, they draw and paint motifs. Roofs are thatched with the dry branches of the stunted khejri tree. Women wear long skirts and blouses, held together with an *odhni* or mantle and these add splashes of colour to an otherwise dull landscape.

In the desert, the camel is man's best friend. A companion on long journeys, it helps navigate, requires little by way of food or water, provides transportation on journeys, and helps till the soil for sowing crops. Its sweet milk is less favoured than a cow's or even a goat's, but provides succour; its hide is turned into *jutees.*

Shortage of water characterises the desert. According to legend, when Rama set out to rescue his abducted wife Sita from the demon king, Ravana, he found himself in front of the sea. So he fitted into his bow an arrow of such power as to consume the sea. At this the sea begged to be saved, but the arrow, once fitted into its slot, had to be fired. Rama, therefore, fired it in the opposite

Top, middle and bottom: *Desert life is harsh, and imposes climatic and social restrictions on people of the Thar. They carry water over long distances, cover their homes with thatch, and plaster them with a paste of cow dung, clay and pieces of hay, and then paint them to bring brightness to their otherwise bleak lives. Most of the work in the home is done by women.* **Facing page:** *For endless miles, the sands of the desert stretch on, shifting dunes rippled by the strond wind. Yet, the desert dweller can navigate his way comfortably, the camel his means of transport, as he charts his journey by the stars at night, or recognises the rare but precious tree that might erupt from the landscape.*

49

to be fired. Rama, therefore, fired it in the opposite direction, and the waters that covered Rajasthan dried up. Though this may be myth, the presence of fossils does much to prove that the land was once, in fact, under water.

Jaisalmer has always been closely linked with Krishna. As a result of having spurred the Pandavas to war with the Kauravas in the Mahabharata, Krishna was cursed by the unfortunate mother of the Kauravas who saw her hundred sons die a terrible death. 'Your sons shall wander the earth, no place their home', she said, and so it came to be. Krishna was forty-sixth in descent from the moon god, and the Yadava rulers in Delhi and in Dwarka were soon overthrown after Krishna succumbed to his injuries. They left for Afghanistan and established a kingdom there, soon to be overthrown.

The Yadavas next migrated to Salihwanpur (now in Pakistan), where Raja Bhatti held sway over a vast empire. Such was his renown that his descendants, thereafter, though Yadavas, have come to be known as Bhattis.

Mahmud of Ghazni attacked the Bhatti citadels and drove them to the desert. Their first capital was Tanot, the second Deorawal, the third Lodurva where they built a city of fabulous wealth. The Bhattis attacked a caravan that belonged to Mohammed Ghori, and carried off horses and priceless jewels. Ghori's revenge was spectacular: he razed Lodurva, and the Bhattis fled once more, leaving behind a few pillars and temples that are a forlorn sign of their once fabulous capital.

Their next capital was to serve the Bhattis the longest. In 1156, following the advice of a hermit, Rawal Jaisal laid the foundations of the fort of Jaisalmer. Though it commands a height, the contoured bastions of the fort camouflage with the sand, so that it surges out of the desert like a mirage, its 'ninety-nine beetling bastions' since celebrated as Sonar Qila or the golden fort.

The location of Jaisalmer was fortuitous. It was on a West Asian trading crossroad. The Rawals offered protection to the merchant community of Jains, and they in turn settled and raised the money for the first of the fort's walls. Later, they added two more concentric walls to make it impregnable. Within the fort, the Rajputs added their Hindu temples, and the Jains their shrines, and along with the habitations of the Muslim stone cutters, Jaisalmer became a truly secular centre. The fort and its shrines were built

between the 12th and the 15th century. The fort is still a living entity today, its apartments occupied by families who have been in residence for centuries. The Maharawals of Jaisalmer were routed in 1295, but though they did not lose their fort, a different tragedy struck them. Apparently, 24,000 women and children embraced *jauhar*, for the *zenana* had not expected a victory. But victorious the rulers did prove, hollow though such a victory may have turned out to be. Incidents such as these are the lifeblood of many of Rajputana's forts.

Within the fort is a Kali temple where ritual sacrifices were performed, specially before a battle. The fort has a Jaisal well, named after the ruler. Since water was Jaisalmer's most precious commodity, Maharawal Garsi ordered the building of a large water tank. Garsisar is still a source of water for Jaisalmer. And around Garsisar, several temples dedicated to the gods who sanctified the settlement were raised. In time to come, a courtesan called Teelon from Jaisalmer became celebrated in the court of Hyderabad (now in Pakistan) and amassed a huge fortune. Once every year, during the rains, she would return to the land of her birth to distribute alms to the poor. On one such visit she ordered the building of a gateway to Garsisar. This was objected to by the citizenrs of Jaisalmer The ruler, they pleaded, could not pass through a gate which had been built from the ill-gotten wealth of a nautch girl.

Teelon then had an idol of Satyanarayan placed above the gate, thus sanctifying it with the presence of god. Not only was the demolition of the gate stayed, the ruler found he could no longer object to its use, and the controversy died down.

Today, Jaisalmer is at the heart of the Desert National Park that aims to help preserve its fragile eco-system, its hardy shrubs, and the great Indian bustard. In the endless sands that are at once awesome and frightening in their expanse, a trained eye will pick out a gazelle, or the swoop of an eagle. But to the visitor, the swooshing silence of the sands and the contours of the dunes have a language uniquely their own.

Ninety nine bastions define the fort that Rao Jaisal built in 1156. The stone battlements rise from a sea of sand. In the 16th century, it was attacked by Pathans who entered the fort on the pretext of their begums wanting to pay a courtesy call on the ranis. The palanquins contained no women, only soldiers, and though they were soon killed, it was not before the ruler had himself taken the life of some of the Bhatti princesses.

Sunset point in Jaisalmer can be seen above the thatched house.

Udaipur today is a delicate city, but it rose from the ashes of war. Udaipur's royals enjoy the highest stature in the land, mainly due to the sacrifices made by the Sisodias in their struggle against the Mughals. Like the Kachchwahas of Jaipur, the Sisodias of Mewar (as the empire was called), trace their origin to Rama. The earliest known history of the clan shows it moving from Kashmir in the Himalayas to the coasts of Gujarat, in the 6th century. Their capital, Vallabhi, was sacked by raiders, but the ruler's pregnant queen escaped as she was away on a pilgrimage. Her son, Guhil, was born in a cave, and left in the safekeeping of the tribal Bhils, while the queen committed sati on her husband's funeral pyre. Guhil grew up among the Bhils and was anointed chieftain. For a while his descendants were known as Gehlots, but they later changed their name to Sisodia. A century later they moved to Mewar. One of them, Bappa Rawal, received Chittaur as his dowry when he wed a Solanki princess. It was to remain with the Ranas of Sisodia from the 8th to the 16th century, but in 1303 it was sacked by the ruler of Delhi, Sultan Alla-ud-din Khilji.

What sparked the dispute was Rana Rattan Singh's beautiful queen, Padmini, whom the Sultan desired though he had only seen her image in a mirror. He sacked the city and took Rattan Singh hostage. To gain time the queen offered to visit the Sultan's camp but a palanquin of soldiers were sent instead. A fierce battle ensued in which seven thousand Rajputs lost their lives. The queen and her entourage committed self-immolation in the ritual *jauhar*.

The second sack of Chittaur took place when it was attacked by Sultan Bahadur Shah of Gujarat, in 1535. Chittaur never recovered from it.

The remaining heir, Udai Singh II, had survived due to the care of a nursemaid, Panna, who brought up the child till he was able to recapture Chittaur, and finally lay the foundation of a new capital, Udaipur. A stupendous palace was built, its severe, forbidding exterior made gentler by the lake besides which it was located. From the sacking of Chittaur had emerged a stronger aesthetic sensibility. The sheer walls of the fortified palace were crowned by an exuberance of domes, arches and turrets, while massive gateways guarded the apartments within.

Rana Pratap succeeded to the throne of Udaipur in 1572, but clashed with Akbar at Haldighati in

Top: The Mor Chowk in Udaipur's City Palace. The enamel peacock is a symbol of the city. *Middle:* The lounge of Shiv Niwas Palace, now a hotel run by the maharana. *Bottom:* A room in the Lake Palace, also a hotel. Coloured glass was often used in palaces to lessen the impact of the summer sun. *Facing page:* In Udaipur, Gangaur procession is taken down the lake, in boats. Here, women wait with idols of Shiva and Parvati on the ghats. *Following pages 56-57:* The Lake Palace, built in the 18th century by Jagat Singh in a fit of pique when his father refused to allow him permission to use his palace.

55

a battle that forms a chapter in every child's history book. Pratap lost, and the Sisodia family once more took to the hills, eating berries and moving at night to defer attention. Finally, Rana Pratap was able to free much of Mewar, and his capital, Udaipur, from the Mughal yoke, but not Chittaur.

Udaipur today houses Krishna Vilas which has the most magnificient collection of miniature paintings. Several of the palaces within the City Palace complex are exquisite. However, Udaipur's *piece de resistance* is the Lake Palace or Jag Niwas, a building in white marble built over an entire island that appears to float on the lake's waters. This was the second of the lake palaces to be built, the earlier being Jag Mandir which had been built by Maharana Karan Singh for his imperial guest, Prince Khurram (later Emperor Shah Jehan). Jag Mandir was named after Karan Singh's son, Jagat, but on one occasion when Karan Singh actually denied Jagat use of the palace for a picnic, he retaliated by building the larger, even more beautiful Jag Niwas. Jag Niwas is a small, but perfect palace, its translucent marble embellished with inlay, and tall, elegant arches framing enchanting views of the lake and the garden courtyards.

Then there is Nathdwara, a centre of pilgrimage for Krishna worshippers, for here an idol of Krishna was brought during the reign of Emperor Aurangzeb to avoid its getting smashed at his behest. And thus was founded the temple of Eklingji where the family deity, Shiva, resides. Further away are the bewitching temples of Ranakpur built by the Jains and ahead, Mount Abu, Rajasthan's only hill retreat, built on the banks of a lake. There are old hunting lodges too, set in spacious grounds, where one can now stay.

There is Kumbhalgarh, a high hilltop fort which is as significant as Chittaurgarh. Built in the mid-14th century by Rana Sangha, Kumbhalgarh is 3,500 feet high and its fortifications envelop homes, palaces, temples and gardens. Reached by a high road, it must have provided a formidable picture in its time. It was captured only once by the combined armies of Emperor Akbar, and of Jaipur and Jodhpur. It stands sentinel over the Aravalli hills, musing over battles past, gazing towards Udaipur, now that the Sisodias are at peace, their battles no longer fought in fields but in court rooms.

Top: *Jag mandir, in the middle of Lake Pichola, close to Lake Palace, was built for visiting prince Khorram (later Emperor Shah Jehan.* ***Middle:*** *The inner courtyard of Shiv Niwas Palace has a swimming pool and a garden which was first planted by the maharanas.*
Bottom: *A view of the City Palace complex, Udaipur.*
Facing page: *Kumbhalgarh, founded by Rana Kumbha, is truly perched atop a hill and ringed by clouds. Rajasthan's most impregnable fortresses, it lost only once, in the seige laid by Akbar.* ***Following pages 60-61:*** *Chittaurgarh is a symbol of Rajput valour. It was from here that the Sisodias ruled, refusing to give in to Mughal power.*

Maharaja Narendra Singh
of **_Bikaner_**
Name of founder: **_Rao Bika_**
Year of foundation: **_1489_**
Name of the clan: **_Rathore_**
Principal fort: **_Junagarh_**
Gun Salute: **_17_**

Maharao Brijraj Singh
of **_Kotah_**
Name of founder: **_Rao Madho Singh_**
Year of foundation: **_1624_**
Name of the clan: **_Hara_**
Principal fort: **_Kotah Fort_**
Gun Salute: **_17_**

Brig. H.H. Sawai Bhawani Singh, MVC _of_ **_Jaipur_**
Name of founder: **_Dhola Rae_**
Year of foundation: **_1150_** _(Amber);_ **_1727_** _(Jaipur)_
Name of the clan: **_Kachchwaha_**
Principal forts: **_Amber, Jaigarh, Nahargarh_**
Gun Salute: 17

Maharana Arvind Singh
of **_Mewar (Udaipur)_**
Name of founder: **_Bappa Rawal_**
Year of foundation: Chittaur **_(728)_**_; Udaipur_ **_(1567)_**
Name of the clan: **_Sisodia_**
Principal fort: **_Chittaurgarh, Kumbhalgarh_**
Gun Salute: 19

Maharaja Brajraj Singh
of **_Kishangarh_**
Name of the founder:
Maharaja Kishan Singh
Year of foundation: **_1609_**
Name of the clan: **_Rathore_**
Principal fort: **_Roopangarh_**
Gun Salute: **_15_**

Maharaja Krishna Chandra Pal *of* **Karauli**
Name of founder: **Dharam Pal**
Year of foundation: **1648**
Name of the clan: **Jadaun**
Principal forts: **Timangarh, Bayana, Karauli Fort**
Gun Salute: **17**

Maharaja Gaj Singh II *of* **Marwar**
Name of founder: **Rao Jodha**
Year of foundation: **1459**
Name of the clan: **Rathore**
Principal fort: **Mehrangarh**
Gun Salute: **17**

Maharaja Mahendra Singh *of* **Mewar** *(Udaipur)*
Name of founder: **Bapp Rawal**
Year of foundation: Chittaur **(728);** Udaipur **(1567)**
Name of the clan: **Sisodia**
Principal forts: **Chittaurgarh, Kumbhalgarh**
Gun Salute: **19**

Maharawal *of* **Jaisalmer**
Name of founder: **Rawal Jaisal**
Year of foundation: **1156**
Name of the clan: **Bhatti**
Principal forts: **Jaisalmer Fort (Sonar Kila)**
Gun Salute: **15**

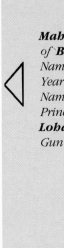

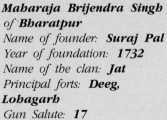

Maharaja Brijendra Singh *of* **Bharatpur**
Name of founder: **Suraj Pal**
Year of foundation: **1732**
Name of the clan: **Jat**
Principal forts: **Deeg, Lohagarh**
Gun Salute: **17**

Rajasthan is as manifestly devout as it is brave. Rajputs and traders have together donated a large number of temples to the desert, which are often as significant as the palaces and forts of the state. Most temples are built in the typical north Indian style with a *shikhara* or spire over the *garbha-griha,* (sanctum sanctorum). Earlier, temples were often placed within the ramparts of forts, since the protection of deities was a warrior's first duty, beyond even his king, or self. Temples which were built at specific locations outside the forts raised defensive fortifications for their protection.

Rajputs worship the very gods from whom they trace their origin. This include Vishnu in all his manifestations. Both Krishna and Rama, from whom the principal clans claim descent are separate incarnations of the same god, Vishnu. Both, significantly, are from a warrior clan, both were kings, able soldiers and leaders of armies. That temples should be raised to worship them is but natural.

However, since the Rajputs were often at war, and death was a constant companion, it was equally natural that they also worship the Lord of Destruction, Shiva. For Shiva is believed to be the fountainhead of all creation and energy. Fertility rituals centre on Shiva, and festivals celebrate the eternal love of Shiva for his wife, Parvati. They are popular symbols of folklore and art, and both the Teej and Gangaur festivals, but specially the latter, pay homage to them. Parvati is also propitiated as Kali, the terrible avenging goddess, specially before riding out to battle. And stories of warriors riding to certain death, wrapped in cloaks of saffron, their foreheads smeared with blood, are no mere legend, for to lose a battle was a betrayal of one's god.

The Rajputs also pray to Sati Matas, or women who have immolated themselves at their husband's funeral pyres. However, not all *satis* were worshipped, though self-immolation to protect one's honour, if a battle was lost, was almost mandatory. It was only those women who became *satis* without compulsion who are still worshipped today, as they were during the medieval ages. *Sati* nowadays is banned by an act of government.

The trading community of Jains have built many of Rajasthan's beautiful temples. The temples are usually of marble, or sandstone and marble, and are decorated with friezes, sculptures and floral motifs carved out of stone. Complete

Above: *An idol from a Jain temple in Jaisalmer. The city had a profusion of Jain temples since most of its trading community which provided its wealth came from the Jain community.* ***Below:*** *A deity in a Hindu temple. The Rajputs prayed to incarnations of Vishnu, but there was also a strong influence of Shaivite worship.* ***Following pages 66-67:*** *In the 1850s, Bharatpur's ruling family created a dam and waterlogged the low-lying land for duck shoots which went on to become famous. With conservation becoming the new mantra, Bharatpur is now a bird sanctuary where waterfowl, such as the rosy pelicans shown here, are the new attraction.* ***Facing page:*** *The Jain temples of Ranakpur, near Mount Abu, are known for their wealth of marble carving, and are an important centre of pilgrimage.*

complexes of temples as in Osian or Ranakpur, or those in Jaisalmer or Bikaner, attest to the tolerance each community had for the other's religion.

Rajasthan's Muslim population too has raised mosques and *pirs* all over the state, and Hindus have been known to seek the benediction of spiritual healing at these places. However, the most famous of the Muslim pilgrimages is to the shrine of Khwaja Moinuddin Chisthi at Ajmer. The Mughals often journeyed here to pray, and following them, the British too retained Ajmer directly under them, though their purpose was more altruistic: modern Western education for the princes of Rajasthan. Another popular Muslim pilgrimage is to the Atarki Dargah of Haminuddin Nagori in Nagore.

A large number of folk heroes too have acquired godhead. The most popular of these is Pabuji, a Rathore warrior whose exploits are now enacted by *bhopas* or priests before a *phad,* or sheet painted with events from his life. Gogaji too was a warrior bestowed by the snake gods with the power to heal those bitten by snakes. Mehaji and his son, Harbhu, are *bhomiyas* or braves who died while saving cattle in a village, while another community, the Bishnois, will willingly lay down its life for the protection of any living being, whether it be a tree, a shrub, a living animal or a bird. Of Ramdeoji, it is said he was born to a childless couple, and spent his life in the service of the people. Even now, when there is a drought, the people train their eyes on the horizon, expecting Ramdeoji to come riding on his white steed, bringing succour with him.

The Rajputs of the state belong to a warrior aristocracy that is peculiar to the Thar. For, these lands were once divided into twenty-two kingdoms, nineteen of which had Rajputs at their head. With exceptions like Shekhawati (which did not constitute an independent kingdom), these kingdoms were based on a system of inheritance where the eldest son gained the title and office.

Preceding pages: *Turning the potter's wheel and giving shape to lumps of clay is a man's job: women can only assist in the process. Ordinary clay pots are beautifully turned and decorated, even though their function is merely practical. Hence, clay pots are piled up outside a kumhar or potter's house which too looks as if it is baked of the same clay as his pots.*

While this led to patricide on occasions, with fathers, sons and brothers battling each other, it also helped to develop the system of inheritance.

Jagirs were feudatory landholdings that were inherited by the younger sons or brothers of the heir (women were also given *jagirs* as personal allowance), and these proved a source of livelihood for them. But unlike most other parts of the country, it was not through farming that the *thakurs* made their money. Instead, these *jagirs* served as defence reservoirs for raising independent armies for the king when required. In return, the state paid them an allowance, exempted them from taxation, or looked after them in some other manner. As a result, most *thikanas* were held by members of the family. And though on numerous occasions *thikanas* realigned forces, for the most part the system helped in strengthening the kingdom.

Little is known of the origin of the Rajputs, their claim to being the progeny of the gods notwithstanding. It is believed that it was in the *agnikul* or great fire of Mount Abu that family lines were created. Most kingdoms were created by chieftains who, through shrewd maneouvrings, brigandage and show of power, were able to offer protection rights to traders and caravans of merchandise. Affluence followed when the princes of the Rajputana houses were able to make peace with the seat of power in Delhi. The Mughals offered them more titles, and were able to influence their durbars, their modes of dress and the structure of kingship.

It is for this reason that every Rajput carries himself with the assurance of being of noble blood, tracing kinship to his gods. This is his inheritance, though times can be hard, and the dry soil can at times make it impossible to eke out a living. Rajputs crowd the military services and have proved, over time, to be among the army's best soldiers.

This page and facing page: *Not only are the women of Rajasthan beautiful, they also wear jewellery literally from head to toe. On the forehead they wear a borla or rakhri, the nose ring is almost mandatory, and of which the Bishnois sport the most beautiful. Their arms are laden with bangles from wrist to shoulder: these graded bangles used to be in ivory, but are now mostly in bone. Necklaces, waist girdles, anklets and toe rings complete the ensemble. Of course, different communities wear different jewellery on various occasions.*

The Brahmins, who elsewhere in India enjoy premier position, are not placed quite as high in Rajasthan. For though the community has been associated with ritual worship, here it was the warrior who was important, and the Brahmins saw it fit to serve the protector. It is perhaps because of this too that the Rajput courts enjoyed a secular rather than a Hindu flavour. This is not to imply that the Rajputs were lesser Hindus. On the contrary, when sailing across the seas, which it was then believed would lead to loss of caste, Maharaja Madho Singh of Jaipur carried his own supply of Ganga water in two huge silver urns on his maiden trip to London.

The Muslims made their first entry into this region in the 12th century, and settled in small pockets in the state. The Shekhawati area was dominated by their presence, since this lay close to Delhi. But with the exception of Tonk, Rajasthan has had no other Muslim kingdom, though there were smaller settlements, such as Loharu, which remained important. The Muslims have always lived in happy co-existence in the state, specially since they never felt threatened by the rulers and their courtiers. They were largely concentrated in cities, and most of them were associated with the arts. So comfortable did they make themselves in the desert that in 1947, at the time of the country's partition, when the Muslim *silvataas,* or stone carvers of Jaisalmer, left for Pakistan, they first built a special Tazia Tower which they dedicated to their ruler before migrating.

The Jats farmers constitute a small percentage of the population, and are chiefly concentrated in areas close to Delhi and Haryana. Rajasthan had two Jat kingdoms, Bharatpur and Dholpur, but it is believed by some that the areas around Churu and in the Shekhawati region were also once held by the Jats. A hard-working, upwardly mobile community, the Jat heritage is closely associated with Haryana and Punjab.

It is the Marwaris who have proved to be Rajasthan's most influential community. The Marwari families, many of them emerging from the Shekhawati, worked in the royal courts as traders, often financing campaigns, as in the case of Rana Sangha's continued battles against the Mughals. However, when the merchants began to venture out with the royal armies to the south and the east, first under Mughal and later British sovereignty, they were able to expand their trading empires. Many of them settled outside Rajasthan, in pursuit of fresh opportunities. Much of modern India's fortunes are held in Marwari investments, and some of the greatest names in Indian industry come from the Marwari community. The Marwaris have also been philanthropists, constructing memorials, temples, schools and hospitals in the towns of their origin.

Rajasthan has been homeland to the tribals for thousands of years, The Rajput kings came to count upon their support, even as they subdued them to establish their own empires. Prime among them were the Bhils and the Minas, the former inhabiting much of south Rajasthan, and closely associated with the fortunes of Chittaurgarh and Udaipur. The Minas once ruled the Aravallis near Jaipur, and to date, Mina tribesmen anoint the Kachchwaha monarch.

Other nomadic and tribal societies include the Gaduliya Lohars, a community of itinerant ironmongers with their colourful carts, and the Garasiyas and Sahariyas. It is from these tribes that the worldwide community of gypsies is believed to have originated.

There are other, special castes that work as potters, cobblers or in any of the intensive craft-related professions, specially weaving, dyeing, and handblock printing, many of them being Muslims.

But apart from all of these are the Bishnois. Committed to the protection of all living things, the Bishnois are the world's first society of conservationists whose women dress in deep earth colours, and whose men wear a distinctive white. They welcome you to their homes with a lick of opium offered from their palms.

No wonder Rajasthan continues to be a mystical, magical land.

Within Rajasthan

What is it that the traveller can look forward to in Rajasthan? As a question, this one is the hardest to answer, for what each one of us sees is what *we* want to see. But—and this is the only certainty—we will all find it to be a fascinating and colourful state, with its historical monuments, its codes of chivalry and honour, and its celebration of life, so unique to the people of this region.

First, then, the land. Rajasthan forms part of the Thar, the great Indian desert. In its true form, this sea of tawny golden sand is best seen in ***Jaisalmer,*** and is next best around ***Bikaner*** and ***Jodhpur***. The three destinations, once independent kingdoms well linked by road, form what is popularly referred to as the desert triangle.

But most of Rajasthan is, in fact, a scrub desert. Here there are scrawny plantations, but if the rains are good, the crop too can be surprising in its bounty. This however is a rare phenomenon. The sandy surface does not retain water, soil is washed away, and with excessive rains, even homes are damaged when sand from under the foundation shifts.

Cutting through Rajasthan, like a pole that has been dropped across it, is the Aravalli range of hills. These hills are forested, and can be lush during the monsoons, though the forests are reduced to a burnt grey and brown in the summer. These hills had provided the base for many of Rajasthan's kingdoms, such as ***Udaipur*** to the south and ***Jaipur*** in the north. They have also provided shelter for sanctuaries, and have the state's only hill resort in Mount Abu.

It is not easy to plan an itinerary for Rajasthan, unless one includes the whole state in one's travels, and the extent of that would require more days than most visitors are likely to have. Elimination of destinations, even small ones, of palaces and forts, is painful indeed. However there are several well-tried itineraries which may be adapted depending on one's own desire to include the region or town of one's preference.

It is most convenient to enter Rajasthan from New Delhi, and the capital of the state, Jaipur, is not only the closest to Delhi but also the most popular tourist city in the state. Jaipur, along with New Delhi and Agra, forms a part of the country's best-known travel circuit called the Golden Triangle. However, the journey between Delhi and Jaipur, which takes half an hour by air, a little over four hours by the Shatabdi Express railway link, and six hours by deluxe bus (a little less in a car), can now be broken into several stages. The old highway between Delhi and Jaipur has a night's halt at ***Sariska,*** a Project Tiger sanctuary, with accommodation in an old hunting lodge, while the current highway has several resorts along the entire route, but a stay at mid-point ***Neemrana*** in a 14th century fortress-turned-heritage hotel can prove the high point of the trip.

A detour on the Jaipur-Delhi or the Bikaner-Delhi highways will take you to the region of ***Shekhawati,*** a pocket of Rajasthan that has come to be characterised by its painted mansions called *havelis.* Some of the fortified settlements of this land provide accommodation in ancestral homes, their atmosphere being far more important than any claims to service that they can provide. A few of these include Castle Mandawa, Dera Dundlod Qila and Castle Mukundgarh. The principal towns in the Shekhawati area include Fatehpur, Ramgarh, Mahansar, Mandawa, Dundlod, Mukundgarh, Jhunjhunu.

Along the Jaipur-Agra highway, **Bharatpur,** a former kingdom, now is best visited for its bird sanctuary where early morning boat rides and bird viewing on bicycles can prove an exhilarating experience. Bharatpur is home to a large variety of resident and migratory waterfowl. Close to Bharatpur is **Deeg,** the former Jat stronghold whose fortified palaces are known for their delicate architectural highlights, and for such romantic pavilions as the monsoon palace where machinery creates the sound of thunder, and coloured fountains play.

From Jaipur, other points of interest are visits to **Kishangarh,** once known for its paintings, and which now has a heritage hotel carved out of the old fort in Rupangarh; **Karauli,** a 'forgotten' kingdom close to the borders of the neighbouring state of Madhya Pradesh, where, in the thick forests, tigers were to be found once; and **Tonk,** the state's only Muslim kingdom at the time of its merger.

From Bombay, a moving and busy cosmopolitan city to **Udaipur,** the entry base to the state and a tranquil settlement where an air of peace reigns over the lakeside capital of Mewar. From Udaipur, visitors can head off towards **Ranakpur** and **Mount Abu,** the prime highlight being trips to Jain temples carved in marble and extremely fluid in their expression. Or they can take a few days to travel to the region's kingdoms of Shahpura, Dungarpur, Pratapgarh and Banswara. The area has still to exploit its tourist potential, so the visitor is likely to be faced with a shortage of accommodation.

The flight that leaves Bombay to connect with Udaipur continues on to Jodhpur. As stated earlier, Jodhpur can be combined with Jaisalmer and Bikaner so that the tourist can experience the Desert Triangle.

The Hadaoti region includes **Bundi, Kotah and Jhalawar,** and in a limited area, includes a wealth of palaces and forts of incredible beauty. Kotah is the base in this region and is fast becoming an important industrial centre.

It goes without saying that winter months are best for discovering Rajasthan. While November to February is the best period, the **best tourist season** is usually considered to be October-March, and has been further extended to include April and September, though these months can be hot. The searing heat of summer, however, arrives in May, when it is madness to venture out during the day, unless one is well protected from the sun. The heat breaks only during the rains, which arrive in mid-June and last through August. However, it will be well to remember that the rains fail Rajasthan often, and if it rains in Jaipur, Jaisalmer may well remain dry. Without the rains, the sultry heat can be unbearable.

Rajasthan has a network of roads, extensive railway lines and airports, and so **getting around** is easy enough. To be totally independent, it is best to go by road. Scheduled bus services ply between all towns, and on longer routes night services are popular.

However, these are likely to be lacking in comfort, and there may be just one or two break-journeys en route at stops where refreshments and toilets can be found. In case of emergencies, the driver will stop along the highway, but you will have to relieve yourself behind some convenient bush (always carry toilet paper).

Rail services are convenient, though with the exception of the Shatabdi and the Pink City express trains these do not have chaircar seating, but berth-style compartments. Reservations are often not easily available (the railways carry a record 11 million people around the country daily), so booking in advance is recommended. Currently, a number of metre gauge tracks are being upgraded to broad gauge for faster, more efficient services. As a result there may be some dislocation of services. However, this is temporary. A unique product is the **Palace on Wheels,** a train tour that was launched in 1982 and consisted of saloons that once belonged to maharajas. This royal train was replaced with a new one, since the old coaches could not carry on indefinitely, but the atmosphere of the original train was retained. Even this is now to be replaced with a Palace on Wheels intended for the broad gauge. The Palace on Wheels itinerary includes all principal towns in Rajasthan, and starts and ends in Delhi. The week-long trip includes extensive sightseeing and all meals.

If you're travelling on your own, the tourist offices in all cities will help make reservations for daily sightseeing trips run by them. Tourist cars are also available in the more important centres. In the smaller towns, such as Shekhawati, Bikaner or Kotah, jeeps may be hired. These usually constitute the cheaper option, but they are less comfortable.

The road between Delhi and Jaipur, or Udaipur and Bombay, is dense with traffic, since these national highways are transportation arteries and a very large number of trucks ply the routes. Overturned trucks and accidents are predictable sights along the way. But in the interior of Rajasthan most highways are fairly open and easy to ply. There remains a certain unpredictability about the roads themselves, which can be wide and very good in some parts, and agonisingly narrow in others. Historically, a large number of roads were laid during years of famine, to provide relief to the people and help them earn some money from the activity of road building. These famine-relief roads tended to be narrow. In recent years they have been broadened. In some parts, such as near Bikaner or Jaisalmer, sandstorms can cover roads as effectively as snow drifts, and have to be cleared. Sandstorms, however, are unknown in the winters, when roads remain clear, with the only deterrent being early morning fog.

In the desert region, **camel safaris** can take you on expeditions on camel-back, away from the towns and roads, through sandy terrain. These safaris can last from a few hours to a few days and if you have the time, are an interesting experience. It may also interest you to know that the large number of camel carts you see on the roads are run on discarded aeroplane tyres.

Near Udaipur, horse safaris are just as popular. And almost all over the state, cycle safaris are organised. Of course, in Jaipur, when visiting Amber, you climb up the steep ramps on elephant back.

Travellers should carry a supply of mineral water with them. The more popular destinations stock mineral water and aereated drinks, but it is safer to carry your own, since there have been distressing reports in the press on bottles of mineral water being adulterated. Aereated drinks include such international brands as Coca Cola, Pepsi, Fanta, Sprite, as well as local brands like Thums Up, Gold Spot and Limca. In case of an emergency, and when very thirsty, it is best to have tea, since this brew is well 'cooked' in Rajasthan. Sugar, tea leaves, lots of milk and water are boiled together, and the sweet tea made from it is good for reviving energy. It is also a good way to meet people, since a cup of tea at a stall breaks the ice very effectively. And you will find that the people can be as friendly as they are hospitable.

Food, now, is another matter. Among the tourist cities, Jaipur is the most cosmopolitan, but even then, the variety of food in restaurants remains limited. You are not likely to find Thai or Japanese or Italian restaurants here, and the few Chinese eateries tend to serve you a Chinese cuisine more suited to local tastes. This is not to say that international cuisine is not available at all. Several restaurants serve a mixed cuisine that could feature fish-n-chips, or pasta, or even pizzas. However, Jaipur does not have speciality international cuisines, and only the luxury hotel restaurants offer you a somewhat limited choice. In smaller cities, it is best to stay off international favourites, since these are rarely what they should be.

Like anywhere else in the world, it is best to stay with the local cuisine, and of that there is a large variety. But a general word of caution first: most local preparations tend to be chilli-hot, and can more than raise the temperature of your body! In restaurants that serve tourists, the spices are usually toned down. But wherever you eat, it will always come in handy to order a side dish of curds or yoghurt, which takes the bite off anything that is hot. A curry made with buttermilk, called *karhi,* is spicy, but digestive, and in fact is the origin of that ubiquitous word 'curry' which has come to imply any gravied preparation in Indian cooking.

Primarily, there are two types of cuisines in Rajasthan, the Rajput and the Marwari. Rajput cooking is non-vegetarian, and was once based on game. This relied heavily on deer (venison), wild boar, hare, partridges, quails and sandgrouse. Since hunting for most of these is now banned, it is only in the open season that one may bag a partridge or two, and the quail you are served in restaurants is likely to be farm raised. Chicken, though widely available, is not popularly used in Rajput cooking, and fish is never used. Though such exotic preparations as stuffed hare cooked in a heated pit of sand are now rarely seen outside of recipe books, the most popular meat preparations are *sula,* or barbecued meat in neat cubes which has been spiced with *kachri,* a cucumber-like vegetable that gives it a distinctive, sour taste, as well as *laal maas* and *safed maas.*

Laal maas is lamb cooked in a rich variety of spices, and using enough red chillies to make your hair stand on end. Though it burns the tongue, its taste is addictive. *Safed maas* is a richer preparation, where lamb is cooked in a coconut gravy, spiced with white pepper, and laced with a paste of cashew and almonds.

Common to both Rajput and Marwari food is the basic *karhi,* dried vegetables called *sangri,* and any number of gram-based curries, such as *gatta, pithor, papar ka saag* and *bhujiye ka saag.* This is usually eaten with *rotis,* or breads made with bajra baked on a griddle. A kedgeree (actually *khichri* or porridge) of bajra and moth, a type of lentil, is also consumed with buttermilk, *karhi,* or just sugar and clarified butter.

Marwari food is vegetarian, richer in spices but less hot, and has oodles of fat. It finds its most characteristic taste in Jaipur, in what has come to be known as *dal-bati-choorma.* What started as picnic food has become a distinctive cuisine of this city. It consists of *batis* or little breads wrapped around clarified butter and baked in a coal fire, which explode when punctured. These are eaten with *dal,* a lentil soup (lentils come in a large variety) along with *choorma,* which in turn is *batis* crushed with sugar or jaggery into a sweet dessert. The three together, simple though they sound, make a very filling meal.

Jodhpur is best known for its *kachoris,* which are hollow dumplings filled with a spicy mixture and eaten with chutney. If you do not like the fire it sets off in your mouth, there is a sweet version of the *kachori,* just one of which is a meal in itself. Bikaner is known for its milk sweets, specially *rasmalai,* and for a savoury snack, *bhujiya.* A large number of shops all over the country claim to sell Bikaneri sweets, for these are as celebrated as Bengali sweets, though their tastes are markedly different.

There is no prohibition in Rajasthan, and liquor is freely available. Most cities have bars, many of them located within hotels. Whereas Jaipur, and the principal hotels in other cities, can serve cocktails, these should be avoided in smaller destinations where it's safest to stick to beer or hard liquors. Wines are difficult to come by. A local liquour, *asa,* is well renowned, but the best stuff is now no longer available, and clones are just not as good. Despite a ban on local breweries, however, there is some brewing of good quality *asa,* so it is worthwhile asking for it, specially around Udaipur, and in Shekhawati's Mahansar.

Accommodation is not a problem in Rajasthan, though there is less than a profusion of chain hotels at the moment. Jaipur obviously has the best accommodation infrastructure, followed by the tourist cities of Udaipur, Jodhpur, Jaisalmer, and so on. In most destinations building activity is underway for more hotels. Unique to the state are its **palace and heritage hotels.** Beginning with the seventies, some of the best palaces of Rajasthan were converted into hotels, allowing visitors to not only sightsee here, but actually stay in them. These are a big attraction, specially since former maharajas and their families continue to reside in one wing of their massive residences. Jaipur's Rambagh Palace and Jai Mahal Palace, Jodhpur's Umaid Bhawan Palace, Udaipur's Lake Palace and Shiv Niwas, Bikaner's Lallgarh Palace and Kotah's Umaid Bhawan are all palace hotels that have contributed to the growth of tourism in these cities.

The next in the rung are heritage hotels usually consisting of reconverted aristocratic homes (no less than palaces) such as Castle Mandawa, or Samode Palace, hunting lodges such as Ramgarh near

Jaipur, or Sariska, or *havelis* such as Piramal. There is a large and growing network of heritage hotels, and they can range from a mere five rooms to over fifty. Since most are run by the families that own them, and are not large enough to be impersonal, their personalised services make them appealing, even when they are not always efficient. They have a charm that few hotels anywhere in the world have. The Heritage Hotels Association in Jaipur or your travel agent can provide you with a list of heritage hotel properties in the state.

Shopping is one of the biggest draws in Rajasthan, and you will find something to buy virtually wherever you are, and generally off the street. In the interiors, you will come across potters sitting by the roadside, silversmiths patterning anklets with bells on them, a stone-carver chiselling away on a statuette, or women drying vividly dyed *odhnis* and sarees in the sun.

Jaipur is the principal centre for shopping. But all towns have comparable arts and crafts they claim as their own. Jaipur and Bikaner, for example, are known for the workmanship of their gold jewellery, and specially *kundan*-work in which uncut stones are set in gold, and their radiance enhanced through the use of lacquer. Jaipur, of course, is the primary centre in India, and only one of two in the world where precious and semi-precious stones are cut and polished by hand. And what a range of jewellery there is to offer, for almost every part of the body ranging from the forehead to the toes!

In Jaipur, marble from Makrana (used for the making of the Taj Mahal) is patterned into statues, and it is said that the marble idols in most Indian temples have been created in Jaipur. But a large number of stones are employed for turning into statuary, as is wood, the latter specially in Udaipur. And Udaipur is also the centre for terracotta art.

Cloth dyeing is practised everywhere, since the local population, despite the easy availability of mill-printed fabrics, continues to favour hand-block printed textiles. Centres flourish in all towns, and the tie-and-dye in Jodhpur has some unusual combinations, while Jaipur's *bagru* and *sanganeri* handblock-printed cottons are the rage of fashion houses not only in the country but all over the world, specially when designed into linen and lightweight quilts. Kotah is known for its Himru or Kotah sarees in cotton, Jodhpur and Nagore for their sturdy *jutees,* while fairs such as Pushkar have become a showcase for the complete arts of the region.

Furniture in the local tradition is manufactured in Shekhawati, while painted furniture can be bought in Kishangarh. Miniature painting is a tradition that has been retained over much of the state, with centres in Jaipur, Udaipur and Kishangarh. In Bikaner, camel skin is painted with gold leaf, and converted into photo frames, lamp shades, miniature bottles and hip flasks.

Festivals abound throughout the year. All-India festivals like Holi and Diwali are celebrated with the rest of the country, while local festivities include those of Gangaur and Teej, when Shiva and Parvati are venerated, their idols taken out in procession through the city streets. All festivals are celebrated with local fervour and a fair-like atmosphere. But it is the *melas,* the fairs themselves, which are the most exciting. The Pushkar fair is already well known, but there are a large number of other *melas* that combine social, religious and trading concerns, and the state tourism department can give you a list of these. In recent years, the Nagaur Cattle Fair has begun to feature on tourist itineraries. At many of these melas, it is still possible to come across anonymous dancers from the Sapera, Langha and Manganiyar communities whose mesmeric music and dancing is the stuff of legends. *Dholis,* or bards, in rich baritones recount the history of the land. In addition to the **melas,** the tourism department organises a large number of annual activities that create more than just a peripheral interest in a destination. Among these are the Elephant Festival in Jaipur, and the Desert Festival in Jaisalmer.

Among the list of fairs organised by the state tourism department or those it actively promotes are the: Nagaur Fair, Nagaur (February); Desert Festival, Jaisalmer (February); Elephant Festival, Jaipur (March); Gangaur Fair, Jaipur (June); Mewar Festival, Udaipur (April); Teej Fair, Jaipur (July-August); Marwar Festival, Jodhpur (October); Dussehra Mela, Kotah (October); Pushkar Fair, Pushkar (November); and Chandrabahga Fair, Jhalawar (November).

Though a desert state, Rajasthan is also surprisingly rich in wildlife, and has a number of **wildlife parks and sanctuaries.** Tigers can still be seen in these parks, as well as the more elusive leopard, but the eco-system also sustains a large variety of deer, monkeys, wild dogs and boar, as well as birdlife. The best known of the state's sanctuaries is **Ranthambore National Park** where some of the most detailed studies on tiger reserves have been conducted. Set in the backdrop of an ancient fortress, the sanctuary is 132 km from Jaipur, and besides the tiger (poaching has taken an immense toll on its population here), has leopards, hyena, wild boar, sloth bear, jackal, and a variety of deer. Another tiger reserve is the **Sariska National Park** where the hilly terrain makes it more difficult to spot this cat, but where the wild dog and deer can be more easily sighted.

The bird sanctuary at Bharatpur, known as the **Keoladeo Ghana National Park,** is best known for its waterfowl, and used to be a base for the study of the Siberian Crane which, however, has failed to be spotted here in the last two years. Besides a very large bird population, the sanctuary also has deer, python, otter, mongoose, fishing cat and jungle cat. The state also has a large number of other sanctuaries for the protection of wildlife, and some of these include the unique Desert National Park spread over the Thar around Jaisalmer, the Jaisamand Sanctuary near Udaipur where crocodiles are commonplace, the Kumbhalgarh Sanctuary, also near Udaipur, and the Tal Chapper Sanctuary in the Shekhawati, which is known for its population of blackbuck. Though there are other sanctuaries, the region between Jodhpur and Bikaner comes under the protection of the Bishnoi community, who are natural conservators and do not allow the killing of wildlife or the felling of trees.

All rights reserved. No part of this publication may be transmitted or reproduced in any form or by any means without prior permission of the publishers.

First Published 1995
© **Lustre Press Pvt. Ltd. 1996**
Reprint 1996
M--75, Greater Kailash-II, Market,
New Delhi-110 048, INDIA
Phones: (011) 6460886/887, Fax: (011) 6467185

Text Editor: Bela Butalia
Concept & Design: Roli CAD Centre

ISBN: 81-7437-035-8

Printed and bound in Singapore

Photo Credits:
Cover: Amit Pasricha

Other photography by
Amit Pasricha, Ganesh Saili, Jean Lois Nou,
Karoki Lewis, Kr. Rajpal Singh, Pankaj Rakesh,
Roli Books Picture Library, Sondeep Shankar,
Subhash Bhargava

Rajasthan—the land of warriors, gorgeous women, royal elegance and vibrant colours. Majestic forts rise from the sands, and ornate palaces throb with a romantic charm, celebrated by throaty ballad-singers. Wild-coloured tie-dyes and handicrafts speak of rare beauty—the swarthy damsel with her unforgettable jingling saunter and haunting eyes.

ISBN: 81-7437-035-8